it's all about school

A Leisure Arts Publication by
Nancy M. Hill of

Acknowledgments

We have made every effort to ensure that these instruments are accurate and complete. We cannot, however, be responsible for human error, typographical mistakes, or variations in individual work.

It's All About School is the third in a series of books written by NanC and Company and published by Leisure Arts, Inc.

Author: Nancy M. Hill
Graphic Artist: Tyler Thomson
Design Director: Candice Snyder
Assistant to Director: Candice Smoot
Cover Design: Maren Ogden
               & Miriam DeRosier
Copy Editor: Dr. Sharon Staples

Layouts:
Front Cover: Main – Leah Fung;
            Corner – Brenda Nakandakari
Back Cover: Camille Jensen,
            Senior Designer

For information about sales visit the Leisure Arts web site at www.leisurearts.com

it's all about school

Yep, that's me! This is our annual 1st day of school photo, back before color film was available to the masses. By the look on our faces at nine and eleven years old my brother and I have definitely outgrown this drill. I can't tell if we are not smiling because:

      (a) School is starting and summer is over

      (b) We don't like our new clothes

      (c) My mother is making my brother and
          I hold hands

      (d) All of the above

Maybe it is just that I don't like my ringlet bangs, and my brother is a little disturbed by his brand new "grow into" Levi's with 6-inch cuffs and a gathered waist. Oh, the things our mothers made us do.

While a lot has changed since this late 1950's photo, one thing has not changed at all. Mothers are still taking photos of their children leaving home on the first day of school.

They are also taking photos of classroom activities, field trips, learning adventures and class parties and trying to find something to do with package A, B or C of the annual school pictures they purchased.

It's All About School is our third idea book designed to spark your creativity and imagination. Our designers have captured their children in a variety of school activities using techniques and designs that can be easily and quickly "lifted" onto your own scrapbook pages. We have provided step-by-step instructions to help you recreate the designs in this idea book.

Reading, writing and arithmetic have never been so fun!

Happy Scrappin',

Nancy

Nancy M. Hill

Table of *Table of* CONTENTS

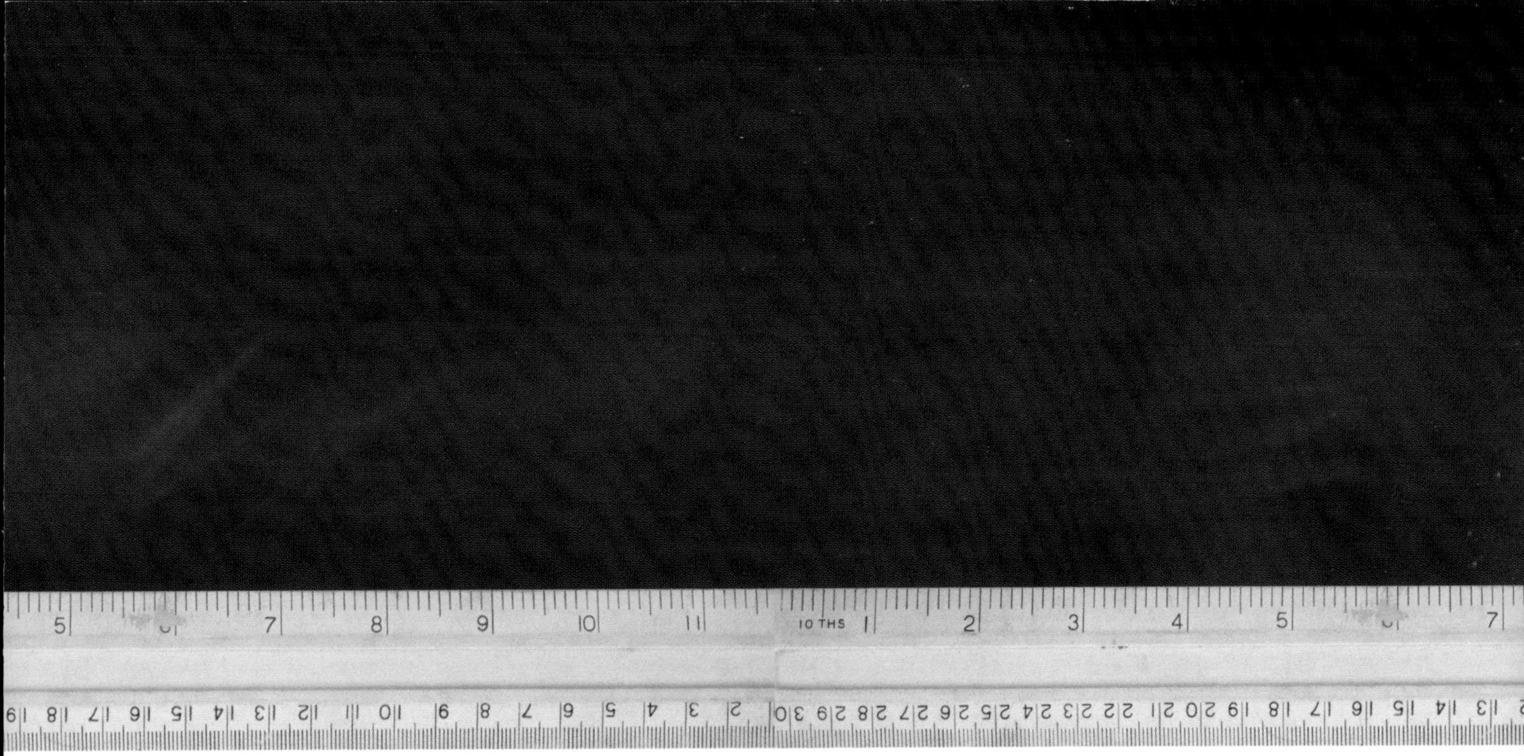

Designer: Wendy Malichio

THE ABC'S OF BACK TO SCHOOL

• create background by adhering black cardstock, gingham ribbon and torn corkboard patterned paper to red cardstock • mat one photo with black cardstock • adhere photos to background • create and print title block paper • attach letter stickers for title • make labels for journaling with label maker • attach pebble letter stickers to metal-rimmed tags • attach tags to layout with brads • embellish layout with paper clips, stickers and string •

Supplies – Cardstock: Bazzill; Cork Paper: Magenta; Apple Seal: Amscam; Ribbon: Offray; Label Maker: Dymo; Letter Sticker: Sticker Studio, Kamset; Rub-on: Making Memories; Tags: Making Memories; Twistal: Making Memories; Metal Letters: Magic Scraps; Pebble Letters: Sonnets; Slide Mount: Two Peas in a Bucket

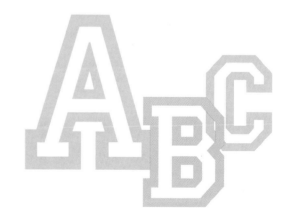

BITTERSWEET TIME OF YEAR

• create background by adhering stripe patterned paper and homemade paper to green cardstock • mat photo with green cardstock, tear bottom edge and adhere to background • attach letter stickers for title • print journaling onto vellum • emboss journaling block while ink is still wet • paint frames with acrylic paint, apply crackling medium and another coat of paint • add twill tape to dry frames • adhere to layout with calendar stickers • stamp leaf image with clear ink onto cardstock and vellum • emboss leaves •
Supplies – Patterned Paper: Chatterbox; Cardstock: Bazzill; Stickers: Creative Imaginations, EK Success

*I have always have mixed emotions this time of year. I want to keep you home and with me forever. But, I know I cannot teach you everything you need to know, so I have to let go. Don't get me wrong, I am ready for more free time, time for me. The house will be tidier, and I'll even get that long needed nap every now and then. My errands will get done more quickly and I won't have to stop at the toy section of the store "just to look", then tell you "no, you don't need another toy". But I will miss you both. I'll miss having you with me, helping me in the kitchen and with chores. I'll miss hearing "Watch me just one more time Mom", or the spontanious hugs & sometimes smooches I get from you. I know, there will always be next summer, and I'll be anxiously waiting for you. Until then, I am going to **ENJOY** every peaceful minute I can scrapbooking!*

Designer: Marsha Musselman

Designer: Camille Jensen

SCHOOL DAYS

• begin with green patterned paper • mat three photos together with dark purple paper, colored with white pencil and smeared with chalk • adhere matted photos to chipboard • create title and accents by stamping letters with white pigment stamp pad onto dark purple cardstock • mat title block and accents with corrugated cardboard • embellish layout with white linen thread •
Supplies – Patterned Paper: Leisure Arts, DCWV; Stamps: Hero Arts

SPECIAL TIPS:
Corrugated cardboard adds texture and dimension to a layout.

BEST PART of a field trip

is riding the **BUS**

October 7, 2002

Children's Inc. Class fieldtrip to **Leads Farm** just north of where we live. The children got an authentic **hayride** with tractor pulling the wagon, saw many animals along the way, stopped at a **pumpkin**/gourd **patch** to pick, then off to the fun **barn** with hay slides and trucks in corn pits and and **petting**/feeding area.

RIDING THE BUS

• create background by adhering yellow cardstock and black mesh to black cardstock • mat photos with black cardstock and adhere to background • create title with black letters and printed cardstock • use black eyelets to adorn the printed cardstock • print journaling highlighting words with color • cut line of school buses from patterned paper • mat buses and journaling with black cardstock and adhere to layout • adhere bus charm to metal-rimmed tag with a pop dot • adhere to layout with string • embellish layout with school bus cut from printed paper •
Supplies – Mesh: Magic Mesh; Stickers: Provo Craft, Two Busy Moms

BUS STOP BEAUTY

• create background by adhering torn magenta paper and ribbon to floral patterned paper • mat photos and adhere to background • reverse print title and cut out with exacto knife •
Supplies – Patterned Paper: Karen Foster; Cardstock: Colormatch; Font: Two Peas in a Bucket Gingersnap

SPECIAL TIPS:
1. Run delicate letters through a Xyron machine.
2. Reverse print title in a graphics program.

bus stop Beauty

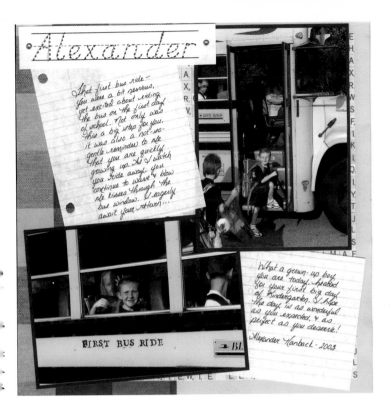

FIRST BUS RIDE

• create background by adhering patterned papers to yellow cardstock • mat photos with black cardstock and adhere to background • cut out child's name from schoolwork for title • attach with gold eyelets • handwrite journaling on notebook paper and adhere to layout • stamp 'first bus ride' onto the photo •

Supplies – Patterned Paper: Leisure Arts, 7 Gypsies; Cardstock: Bazzill

PHOTO TIPS:

Photos are often the focal point of a page. Improving your photos is one of the best ways to improve your scrapbook pages. Our number one photo suggestion is to keep a camera with you at all times to capture unexpected, wonderful moments. Here are some additional suggestions to help improve your photo taking abilities.

POSING

• Take photos that are not posed to give variety and a natural look to your photos. Allow people (especially kids) to be themselves.
• If a posed look is desired, put your subjects at ease by giving them suggestions for poses or providing them with a prop.
• Crop in close and focus in on a detail or object.
• Bring the subject in close to the camera when you are taking a photo of a person in front of a large object (a building or landscape, etc.).
• Photograph the little things that aren't typically photographed!

LIGHTING

• Get out of the bright sunlight and keep the sun out of your subject's eyes. The best light is early in the morning or just before the sun goes down. If you can't get out of the bright light, find shade. If there's no shade, use a flash.
• The most flattering lighting is low-contrast lighting; it makes people look thinner and younger with clearer skin. The larger the source of light, the lower the contrast will be (window light is more flattering than a flashlight).

FILM

• Low-speed film requires more light than high-speed film to be exposed properly, but is less grainy, and the colors are more saturated. A good all-purpose film speed is 200 or 400.
• Color negatives can be printed in color, black and white or sepia, whereas, black and white negatives can only be printed in black and white or sepia.
• All color and most black and white photos are printed on resin-coated paper (RC) and will last 30-60 years before fading or color-shifting, if stored properly. If you have an important photo you would like to last for hundreds of years, have a fiber-based black and white print made.
• Have your film developed promptly and keep it out of the heat.

IMAGINE THE POSSIBILITIES

• begin with textured cardstock for background • frame photo with photo mat • attach fibers that reach around back of layout to framed photo • mat small photo with corrugated cardboard and adhere all photos to background • create title by painting metal letters and tag with acrylic paint • print journaling onto collage paper and adhere to layout • stamp date onto background • embellish layout with fibers, charm, safety pin and raised paper circles •

Supplies – Patterned Paper: Legacy Collage; Cardstock: Bazzill; Fibers: Trimtex; Metal Letters: Making Memories; Metal Tag: Making Memories; Date Stamp: Making Memories

SPECIAL TIPS:

Layer the metal tag and letters with different colors. When each coat is dry, sand it to reveal the color beneath.

ALL FOR YOUR VERY FIRST DAY OF SCHOOL

• create background by adhering torn yellow patterned paper to red patterned paper • mat photos with patterned paper and adhere to background • handwrite journaling onto white cardstock • accent journaling with letter stickers • attach school-themed stickers onto 1" white squares matted with red cardstock • adhere embroidery floss over yellow paper • attach squares over floss with pop dots • embellish layout with swirl clips •

Supplies – Patterned Paper: Provo Craft; Floss: DMC; Stickers: Provo Craft, Mrs. Grossman's; Swirl Clips: Making Memories

SPECIAL TIPS:
Place swirl clips on layout so the largest amount of swirl is visible.

FIRST DAY AT PRESCHOOL

• create background by attaching homemade paper and trimmed black cardstock to checked paper with photo corners • mat photo with cardstock and adhere to background • create title with letter stickers and alphabet stamps • adhere part of title on vellum envelope holding journaling tag • handwrite journaling onto white cardstock • embellish journaling block with eyelet and ribbon •

Supplies – Patterned Paper: Frances Meyer

SPECIAL TIP:
1. Make apple background from child's finger-painting artwork.
   a. Scan artwork and save as a TIFF file.
   b. Use photo-editing software to cut and paste specific parts of artwork you wish to duplicate.
2. Enhance with polka dots or other accents and print onto photo paper.

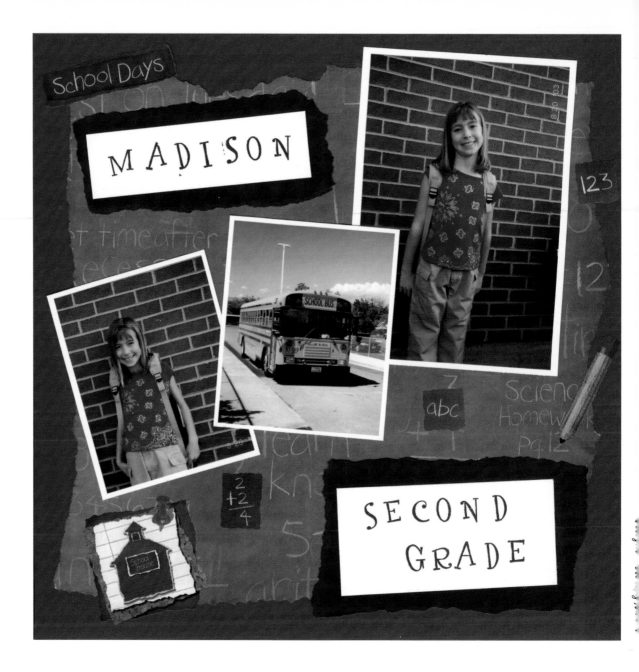

School Days

MADISON

SECOND GRADE

2+2=4

SECOND GRADE
• create background by adhering torn patterned paper to red cardstock • mat photos with white cardstock and adhere to background • stamp title on white cardstock and mat with torn black cardstock • adhere title to background • embellish layout with school stickers •
Supplies – Patterned Paper: Karen Foster Designs; Stickers: Karen Foster Designs

BRAVE JAMESON

• create background by adhering piece of patterned paper and gingham ribbon to black cardstock • mat photos • print title and journaling onto white cardstock • ink edges of white cardstock and adhere to background • cut strips of patterned paper and adhere to layout over journaling block • adhere letter stickers for name • adhere photos to layout • embellish layout with die cut heart and floss •

Supplies – Patterned Paper: 7 Gypsies, KI Memories; Cardstock: Bazzill; Stickers: Rebecca Sower, Provo Craft; Ribbon: Ofrey; Floss: DMC; Ink: Colorbox; Stamp: 2000 Plus; Font: Harting

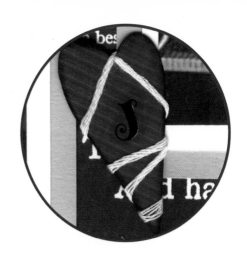

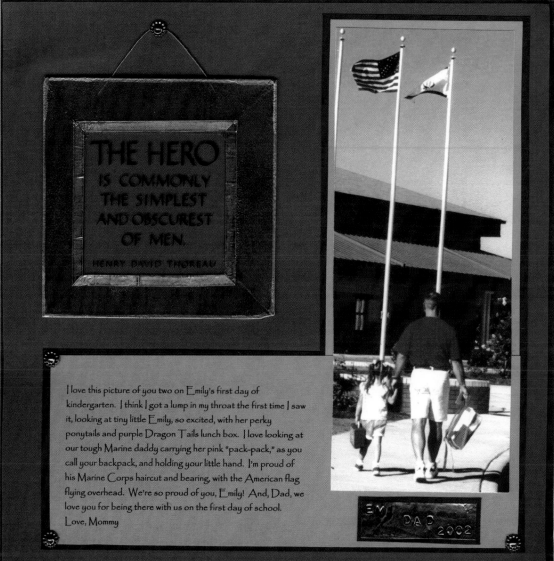

THE HERO
IS COMMONLY
THE SIMPLEST
AND OBSCUREST
OF MEN.

HENRY DAVID THOREAU

I love this picture of you two on Emily's first day of kindergarten. I think I got a lump in my throat the first time I saw it, looking at tiny little Emily, so excited, with her perky ponytails and purple Dragon Tails lunch box. I love looking at our tough Marine daddy carrying her pink "pack-pack," as you call your backpack, and holding your little hand. I'm proud of his Marine Corps haircut and bearing, with the American flag flying overhead. We're so proud of you, Emily! And, Dad, we love you for being there with us on the first day of school.
Love, Mommy

designer: Melissa Smith

THE HERO

• create background by adhering green cardstock to blue cardstock • print photo in panoramic setting • create title frame by attaching sticker to a piece of glass • attach strips of foil tape as frame around sticker and then emboss with blue and silver embossing powder • attach to background with nail head and string • print journaling onto cardstock, adhere photo to journaling block and mat with blue cardstock • attach to background with nail heads • stamp name and date onto metal strip and fill in stamps with blue glass paint • mat with blue cardstock and adhere to background •
Supplies – Metal: ArtEmboss; Metal Stamps: Foofala; Foil Tap: Leave Memories; Font: Papyrus

SPECIAL TIP:

Incorporate glass into your scrapbook pages for a unique look. Try embossing, etching, painting and stamping glass.

BEAUTIFUL
Aspire
Imagine
achieve
Dream
Believe

Take a Look Through My Eyes

Kelly...You are ready, I am not. Your first day of kindergarten and I see my baby, in typical style leading the pack, full of confidence and curiosity. You would be amazed at the other wonderful things I see in you...just take a look through my eyes. I love you my Bella. mommy

THROUGH MY EYES

• create background by adhering trimmed patterned paper to blue cardstock • mat large photo with blue cardstock • frame small photo with metal frame • print title onto vellum, trim and attach to background over large photo with silver eyelets • tear vellum to show child • print journaling onto vellum and adhere to background • attach metallic accent words to background with silver eyelets • adhere framed photo to layout • embellish layout with metal stars and fibers •

Supplies – Cardstock: DCWV; Vellum: DCWV; Metallic Words: DCWV; Metallic Accents: DCWV; Font: Scriptina, Andale Mono

KINDERGARTEN STRIDE

• begin with quadrant paper for background • double mat photos and zig-zag stitch with sewing machine • adhere photos to background with foam tape • adhere metal letters for title • print journaling onto white cardstock • double mat journaling and poem block and zig-zag stitch • embellish layout with gingham ribbon and small and large mosaic stickers •

Supplies – Patterned Paper: The Robin's Nest; Cardstock: Bazzill; Metal Letters: Making Memories; Tile Stickers: Sticko; Poem Block: The Robin's Nest

SPECIAL TIP:
Coordinate page elements and embellishments with colors in photo.

First Day

Your first day of kindergarten was much more exciting to you than to me. Your teacher, Mrs. Davis, let you pick your chair and a cubby for your Hulk back-pack. As I left the school, feeling un-needed, I was a bit teary but you didn't see. My baby boy is in real school now.

You left for school
In a grin so wide
Strutting a new
Kindergarten stride
You walked away,
Backpack in tow.
It was hard for me
To let you go...
Jackie A. Colton

Designer: Brenda Nakandakari

MONTESSORI A GREAT START

• create background by stitching trimmed and torn tan cardstock to red cardstock • mat photo with blue cardstock and adhere to background • create title by matting punched squares from red cardstock with navy cardstock • hand write letters in each square and adhere to page • hand write journaling on tan cardstock • highlight words and edges with chalk • create sign with chalked cardstock and hemp • hang from button sewn to page • embellish layout with school stickers •

Supplies – Cardstock: DCWV; Chalk: Craf-T; Stickers: Creative Memories

ATTITUDE, ATTITUDE, ATTITUDE

• begin with checked paper for background • mat picture with mulberry paper, frame and adhere to background • print title onto vellum and mat with white cardstock • run sheer ribbon through metallic accent and adhere to layout • adhere journaling to page • embellish layout with burlap, button and pearl cotton •

Supplies – Patterned Paper: DCWV; Vellum: DCWV; Mulberry Paper: DCWV; Metallic Words: DCWV; Font: Two Peas in a Bucket Falling Leaves

CLASSMATES

• create background by adhering home-made striped paper (run compressed sponge with re-inkers along the edge of a ruler to make straight lines) to navy cardstock • mat photo with white cardstock and attach to background with photo corners from red cardstock • tear piece of white cardstock for title and sponge edges with navy blue ink • attach title to tag made from red cardstock • embellish tag with sponged metal-rimmed tag, buttons and red and blue raffia • adhere metal quote to layout •

Supplies – Cardstock: Close to my Heart; Re-inkers: Close to my Heart; Buttons: EK Success; Metal Quote: Making Memories

Designer: Lisa Lang

JIMMY NEUTRON BACKPACK

• create background by attaching torn mustard cardstock to brown cardstock with gold brads • adhere natural netting to mustard cardstock • mat photos with mustard cardstock and torn mulberry paper • print journaling onto mustard cardstock and cut to tag shape • tear edge, attach mustard colored eyelet and fibers and adhere to background • attach charms with gold mini brads to tag • adhere cutouts to cardstock and mulberry paper and adhere to page •

Supplies – Cardstock: Bazzill

SPECIAL TIPS:
Wet edges of cut mulberry paper to make torn edges more controllable.

Designer: Camille Jensen

MEG'S PRESCHOOL

• begin with green patterned paper for background • mat photos with pink mulberry paper and frame with ribbon and trim • create title by stamping letters with clear resist ink onto glossy coated paper • sponge letters with ink from a kaleidoscope pad • cut out letters and adhere to layout • print journaling onto vellum using different fonts • ink the back of the vellum with fingertips and kaleidoscope ink pad • adhere vellum to white tag • attach to layout with green brad •

Supplies – Patterned Paper: Leisure Arts; Mulberry Paper: DCWV

THE GRADUATE

• create background by adhering trimmed patterned paper to black cardstock • mat photo with red cardstock and adhere to background • attach alphabet stickers and graduation die cut for title • print journaling onto white cardstock and adhere to background • attach premade graduation tag to layout • adhere 3-D graduation cap sticker to layout •

Supplies – Patterned Paper: Colorbok; Cardstock: Bazzill; Tag: EK Success; Stickers: Darice; Font: Two Peas in a Bucket Flea Market

SPECIAL TIPS:

1. Use the Xyron machine to apply adhesive to delicate letters.
2. The pre-made tag made this an easy project and gave it a great finishing accent.

Designer: Kim Kaiser

Designer: Debbie Coe

GOOD LUCK, GUPPIES

• create background by stitching trimmed blue paper and gingham ribbon to red cardstock • double mat photos with white and red cardstocks and adhere to background • cut out and adhere graduation title • print journaling onto vellum and adhere with glue dots topped with alphabet brads • thread alphabet beads with wire and curl the edges • adhere beads over title and onto vellum with graduate sticker • attach vellum with flat red eyelets • apply shine to graduation cap and adhere to layout • embellish layout with graduation tassel •

Supplies – Title: Li'l Davis Designs; Stickers: Provo Craft, Me and My Big Ideas; Shine: Paper Glaze

SPECIAL TIPS:

Before sewing your layout paper, run two sheets of scrap paper through your sewing machine. Adjust the tension and stitch size as needed before sewing your layout paper.

Today I woke up chanting
"I will not cry! I will not cry!"

Today you woke up very
excited about getting on the
big yellow school bus that
would take you to your first
day of Kindergarten.

Today I counted the minutes
until I could go back to the bus
stop and see you again.

Today you got off the bus
with the biggest smile on your
face and could not wait to tell
me all about your teacher,
classroom, and new friends.

Today I breathed a sigh of
relief.

Designer: Tracey Pagano

I WILL NOT CRY

• create background by adhering torn and rolled white cardstock to green cardstock • frame small photo and adhere all photos to background • stamp title with lettering stamps onto small tags • tie embroidery floss through each tag and knot • adhere tags to background with pop dots • print journaling block onto vellum and adhere to background • stamp date onto background • rip vellum out of metal tag and adhere to page • adhere bus charm to center of metal tag •
Supplies – Stamps: Hero Arts; Tags: Paper Reflections; Floss: DMC; Metal Tag: Making Memories; Bus Charm: Treasured Memories; Ink: Close to my Heart

Kinder

Designer: Maegan Hall

LAUGH, DISCOVER, PLAY

• create background by inking green patterned paper •
mat photo with cardstock and crumpled and inked
brown patterned paper • adhere photo to background •
reverse print name onto cardstock and cut out • attach
three word stickers to background over oval designs •
print journaling onto clear vellum • tear top and bottom
edges and ink • attach to layout with distressed punched
squares and mini brads • attach distressed, punched
squares to each corner of the photo mat •
Supplies – Patterned Paper: Leisure Arts; Stickers: Bo Bunny;
Brads: All the Extras

SPECIAL TIPS:
Crumple cardstock or paper
with water, flatten paper and
dry with an iron or heat
embossing tool. The crumple
gives the paper a leathery and
aged look.

FIRST DAY OF KINDERGARTEN

• create background by adhering plaid paper and box
paper to daisy background • mat photos with cardstock
• rip out center of cardstock to create frame for one
photo • fold and chalk edges and make fake stitches with
pen • print title onto computer paper and use as template to cut out title • run letters through a Xyron
machine and adhere to vellum • outline letters with pen
and adhere vellum to background • finish title with
stamps and attach to layout with eyelets • print journaling, chalk edges and attach with eyelets •
Supplies – Patterned Paper: Chatterbox; Cardstock: Crafter's
Workshop; Flowers: Jolee's By You; Eyelets: Making Memories;
Stamp: PSX; Fonts: Tintibulation, Cheri

SPECIAL TIPS:
1. If a photo has dead space in
   the background, frame it
   with a torn mat.
2. Let your child journal
   his/her first day of school
   to have two different
   points of view.

16

Designer: Valerie Barton

BIG SCHOOL IS COOL

• begin with blue cardstock for background • triple mat photos • create bulletin board for title by framing corkboard with strips of corrugated paper • print title onto white cardstock using Primary Lined font • cut title into strips to look like sentence strips • adhere die cuts to title • adhere title block to layout • print journaling and date onto vellum using Kidscript font • create folder by adhering vellum to green cardstock • embellish layout with vellum tag die cut, pre-made tag and crayons •

Supplies – Patterned Paper: Paper Adventures; Corkboard: Magic Scraps; Corrugated Paper: Paper Reflections; Tag: Making Memories; Die Cut: AccuCut; Crayons: Jolee's By You; Fonts: Primary Font III, Kidscript

Designer: Leah Fung

KINDERGARTEN 2003

• create background by adhering check, red, and cork patterned papers to blue cardstock • adhere two small triangles to bottom corners of background • mat photo with black cardstock and attach to background with eyelets • attach letter stickers for title • print journaling onto patterned paper and attach to cork paper with alphabet brad • attach bookplate to cork paper with two brads • embellish layout with paper clip, die cut and alphabet stickers •

Supplies – Patterned Paper: Leisure Arts; Brad: Making Memories; Die Cut: Creative Imaginations; Stickers: Colorbok

Designer: Leah Fung

CHAPTER TWO

• create background by attaching torn and crumpled blue paper and checked paper to brown cardstock with silver brads • mat photos with cardstock and adhere to background • trace edge of letter die cuts with metallic pen for title • adhere to background over red paper blocks with foam tape • handwrite journaling onto cardstock and draw line around edges with metallic pen • adhere large journal box to layout • adhere small journal box to metal tag • insert metal chain and adhere tag to layout with foam tape • attach strip of cork to layout with eyelets and glue dots • attach three photos to corkboard with brads • string alphabet beads onto wire and curl ends with wire pliers • adhere beads to layout • adhere homemade booklet to layout •

Supplies – Patterned Paper: K & Company; Brads: Making Memories; Title: Provo Craft; Metal Tag: Making Memories; Eyelets: Making Memories

JACOB GOES TO SCHOOL

• create background by adhering chalkboard patterned paper and a strip of black cardstock to red cardstock • mat picture with black cardstock and adhere to layout • print journaling block onto white cardstock and mat with black cardstock • chalk and outline journaling block • adhere journaling block to background • bead name and letters onto black wire with red divider beads • adhere beads to journaling block • handwrite onto metal tag to finish title • chalk tag and attach to layout with red brad • attach red eyelets to four metal tags • chalk tags and adhere school buttons to tags • hang three tags from red brads with white floss • attach two red eyelets to photo • attach fourth tag to photo with string •

Supplies – Cardstock: Paper Loft; Tags: Making Memories; Buttons: Dress it Up; Eyelets: Making Memories; Brads: Doodlebug; Alpha Beads: Western Craft; Beads: Western Craft; Wire: Western Craft; Floss: DMC

UNIQUE EMBELLISHMENTS

There are countless embellishments to use on your scrapbook pages. Just go into a local scrapbooking store and you will be amazed by the possibilities. These embellishments have not only made scrapbooking easier, but more fun.

Here is a list of some embellishments to spark your interest and give you ideas: beads, metal letters, metal looking letters, rocks with or without letters, wood in multiple designs, paints (watercolor, acrylic, glass paint, etc), fibers, twines, watch glass, rub-ons, wax seals, diamond glaze, heat embossing, cold embossing, papers, sandpaper, cardstock, rice, corrugated cardboard, handmade paper, modeling paste, shrink art plastic, transparencies, screen material, mesh, ribbons, buttons, stamps and inks, walnut ink, lazertran paper for decals, envelopes of every shape and material, old type writer keys, feathers, wire, glitter, paper clips, tags, clay, and stickers made to look like most of these things without the bulk!

Scrapbooking stores are not the only place to find embellishments. Try hardware, fabric, thrift and jewelry stores as well. It is fun to use embellishments that you would not expect to find on a scrapbook page. Don't be overwhelmed by all the possibilities, just use what you like, try new things and enjoy the process.

ALL I REALLY NEED TO KNOW I LEARNED IN KINDERGARTEN

• begin with textured cardstock for background
• print journaling onto textured cardstock •
enlarge photo to 5x7 and punch two holes in
top • fit fiber through holes and knot at ends •
adhere to background with silver star brad •
Supplies – Fiber: On the Surface; Fonts: CK Primary,
Penmanship Print, Times New Roman, Californian FB

SPECIAL TIPS:
Simple pages really focus on
the child.

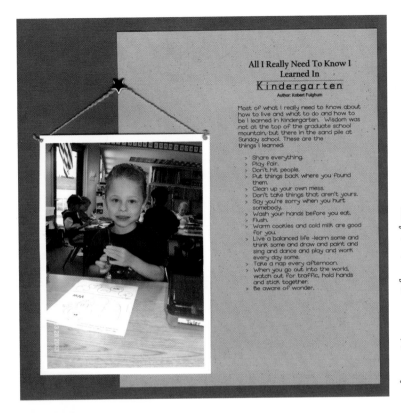

All I Really Need To Know I
Learned In
Kindergarten
Author: Robert Fulghum

Most of what I really need to know about
how to live and what to do and how to
be I learned in Kindergarten. Wisdom was
not at the top of the graduate school
mountain, but there in the sand pile at
Sunday school. These are the
things I learned.

> Share everything.
> Play fair.
> Don't hit people.
> Put things back where you found
  them.
> Clean up your own mess.
> Don't take things that aren't yours.
> Say you're sorry when you hurt
  somebody.
> Wash your hands before you eat.
> Flush.
> Warm cookies and cold milk are good
  for you.
> Live a balanced life -learn some and
  think some and draw and paint and
  sing and dance and play and work
  every day some.
> Take a nap every afternoon.
> When you go out into the world,
  watch out for traffic, hold hands
  and stick together.
> Be aware of wonder.

Designer: Tracy A. Weinzapfel Burgos

WOW, THIS IS SCHOOL

• create background by attaching torn
patterned papers and check patterned
paper to black cardstock with silver snaps
• adhere photos to page • attach library
card and envelope to background with
eyelets for title • create labels with label
maker and attach to layout • stamp journaling onto library card with black ink •
attach alphabet stickers onto six cardstock squares • draw line around edges
with black pen • mat squares with patterned paper and cardstock • adhere to
page with foam tape •
Supplies – Patterned Paper: Leisure Arts;
Stamps: Hero Arts; Stickers: Leisure Arts; Snaps:
Making Memories; Eyelets: Making Memories;
Label Maker: Dymo

Designer: Leah Fung

Designer: Brenda Nakandakari

GROOVY KELLY

• create background by adhering trimmed and torn patterned paper, yellow cardstock and flower stickers to green cardstock • mat photo with green cardstock and frame with border stickers • adhere photo to background • mat a yellow tag with green cardstock • handwrite journaling and attach heart sticker to corner • embellish tag with wired beads and fibers • adhere to layout • thread seed beads with wire and make curly-q • adhere to flower centers • embellish layout with heart stickers •
Supplies – Patterned Paper: Leisure Arts; Cardstock: DCWV; Tag: DCWV; Stickers: Leisure Arts

FIRST GRADE

• create background by adhering strips of purple cardstock and vellum to blue cardstock • tear holes in purple cardstock for lettering and flowers • frame photo with torn, patterned vellum and chalk edges • attach to layout with fibers strung through eyelets • mat class photo and attach to layout with paper clips attached to fiber • attach eyelet letters for title • print name, age and date and adhere to book plate • attach eyelet flowers with fibers as stems • chalk layout for depth •
Supplies – Vellum: Fiskars; Eyelet: Making Memories; Fiber: Fibers by the Yard; Chalk: Craf-T

Designer: Jeniece Higgins

INSPIRE. CREATE. DREAM.

• begin with blue cardstock for background • double mat photo with patterned and textured paper • print journaling with Garamouche font onto white cardstock • adhere journaling to background • tear patterned paper and adhere to background • attach photo to layout with silver snaps • attach stickers to metal-rimmed tags • thread beads onto craft thread and tie to rectangular tag • adhere tag to layout • create booklet with white cardstock strips folded in half • cover booklet with blue cardstock • tie booklet together with craft thread and one bead • attach square tag to cover of booklet • adhere photos and journaling inside booklet • embellish layout with stickers, snap, and word eyelet • Supplies – Patterned Paper: Karen Foster, Creative Imaginations; Stickers: Creative Imaginations; Word Eyelet: Making Memories; Beads: On the Surface; Tags: Making Memories; Font: Garamouche

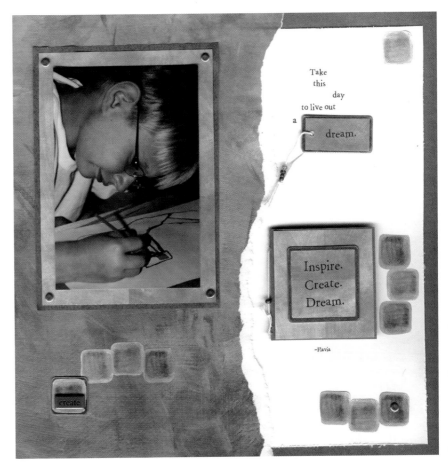

Designer: Dee Gallimore-Perry

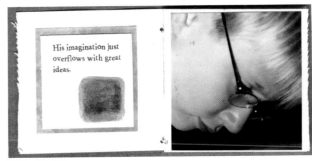

22

JAKE — OUR SECOND GRADE BOY

• begin with green textured cardstock stenciled with a marker for background • frame photo with cut strips of copper • use metal stamps to stamp name, grade and teacher onto frame • ink copper with fingers • attach frame together with large snaps and to background with glue dots • mat class picture with tan and green cardstock and corrugated cardboard • ink edges and adhere to background • print journaling onto light yellow vellum and sew to patterned paper • rub pre-made tag with black, green and orange ink pads • handwrite journaling with calligraphy pen • embellish tag with cut copper and cotton string aged with walnut ink • adhere tag, journaling and string to layout •

Supplies – Stamp: Foofala, Staz-On; Tag: DCWV; Marker: Versamark

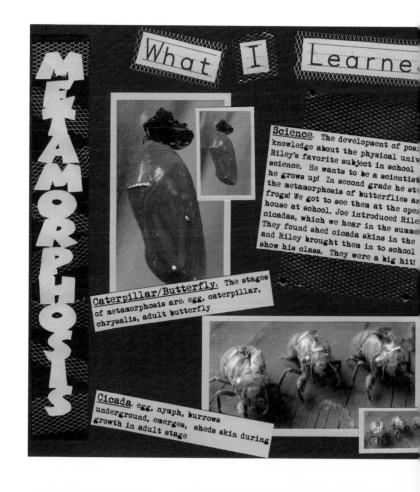

FALL BACK TO SCHOOL

• create background by attaching torn blue vellum and white cardstock to red cardstock with silver brads • single and double mat photos and adhere to layout • frame small photo • attach two black eyelets to bottom of one photo • create title with alphabet stickers and cursive handwriting • embellish title with red buttons • print journaling onto vellum • double mat and attach to layout with silver brads • adhere framed photo to journaling block • adhere school stickers to vellum metal frames • replace string in frames with metal chains • thread through photo eyelets • embellish layout with raffia bow •
Supplies – Patterned Paper: Leisure Arts; Stickers: Leisure Arts; Metal Chain: Leisure Arts; Tags: Making Memories; Metal Frame: Making Memories

Designer: Erin Madsen

Designer: Terri Botwinski

METAMORPHOSIS

• create background by attaching mesh to black cardstock with silver brads • enlarge and change color of photos, mat and adhere to background • reverse print title and cut out letters • print rest of title with Primary Lined font • adhere title to background over mesh • print journaling with Typewriter font and adhere to layout • embellish layout with magnifying glass and butterfly •
Supplies – Cardstock: Bazzill; Fonts: Penmanship Print, Bomk Letters, Mom's Typewriter

COOL CONFIDENCE

• create background by adhering blue patterned paper and torn green patterned paper to white cardstock • mat photo and adhere to background • print title and journaling onto vellum, tear and attach to layout with eyelets • thread ribbon through eyelets • adhere torn patterned paper and beaded and curled wire to a vellum metal rimmed tag • embellish tag with fibers and a green, wood tile • adhere tag to layout • stamp dragonfly image onto white background • stamp one dragonfly image onto scrap piece of paper, scan, enlarge and print onto back of blue patterned paper • cut out and adhere to layout over sheer fabric •

Supplies – Patterned Paper: Making Memories, Karen Foster; Vellum: Paper Adventures; Tag: Making Memories; Green Wood Square: Gotta Notion; Wire: Artistic Wire; Stamps: Stampin' Up; Fiber: Fibers by the Yard; Beads: All the Extras; Eyelets: All the Extras

TRANSPARENCIES/VELLUM

Transparencies are a great medium for titles, journaling, graphics and even photos, and are so easy to use. A transparency can give any look you are trying to create from old fashioned to shabby chic. The key to creating the perfect look is in the font and background selection. To make a transparency, just measure where the title or journaling should be on the layout, print or handwrite onto the transparency and attach it to the layout. You can either attach pieces of the transparency to the layout or the entire transparency as an overlay. You can also add variety to your transparencies by printing graphics and photos, drawing with markers and by printing text in color. Printing your photos onto a transparency gives them a great translucent quality.

Vellum is also a wonderful choice for overlays, titles, journaling and quotes. Vellum comes in many different weights, colors, designs and textures. Don't be afraid to play around with the different options to see which you like best. Most vellum will work fine with an ink-jet printer but does even better with a laser printer.

Vellum is an excellent material for representing water. Choose water colored vellum, rip the edges and layer with the same color or coordinating colors. Vellum's translucent quality also gives an ethereal and pure look to the soft and heavenly qualities of a newborn babe, child and bride.

The best glue to use in adhering transparencies and vellum to a layout is none at all. Try attaching them with brads, eyelets, stitches, nail heads, fibers, or even wedging an edge under another element on a page with a drop of glue. Vellum tape can be used but usually shows through the vellum. You can use a Xyron machine to adhere transparencies and vellum to a layout, but be aware that it does change the look of the medium.

FIRST DAY OF 4TH GRADE

• create background by adhering red vellum to stripe patterned paper • adhere photo to background • print journaling onto white cardstock • draw line with loops above title and adhere journaling block to background • embellish layout with pencil sticker •

Supplies – Patterned Paper: Leisure Arts; Cardstock: Bazzill; Stickers: Paper Bliss

SPECIAL TIPS:

There is an endless supply of fonts to choose from on the computer. They can be found in software programs and on the Internet. Try to match a font with the event you are trying to describe. It is also fun to use many different fonts on one layout.

$3 \times 4 = 12$

First Day of 4th Grade

It is hard to believe that you are already a 4th grader! The time has flown by quickly. This year you have Mrs. Starks, which is the same 4th grade teacher that your brother had a few years ago. Her room is bright and colorful, and filled with lots of interesting books and games. You were so excited about getting back to school to visit with your friends. What a great school year this will be!

Domonique   August 11th, 2003

Designer: Shyne Hanback

School Day Memories

SCHOOL DAY MEMORIES

• create background by adhering black paper and attaching cork patterned papers to brown cardstock with eyelets • mat one photo and adhere all photos to cork paper with brads • attach alphabet letters for title • print journaling onto white cardstock, punch holes, ink edges and attach to corkboard with brads • create booklet by backstitching pages and cover together • ink edges of book title and adhere to cover • adhere cut brad to cover with glue dot • fill pages with photos and journaling •

Supplies – Cork Paper: Magenta; Stickers: Making Memories; Brads: Cut-it-Up, Deco; Frame on Book: Sierra Print Artist; Floss: DMC; Chalk: Craf-T; Font: Two Peas in a Bucket Chicken Shack

Designer: Betsy Sammarco

SPECIAL TIPS:

1. Using products that resemble a bulletin board and chalkboard enhances the school theme.
2. A mini book is a great way to add more school photos to a layout.

BACK TO CLASS

• create background by cutting 'back to class' overall in half and adhering to top and bottom of cork patterned paper • mat photo and attach to background with brad • have child journal their school experience and attach to layout • embellish layout with ruler ribbon, pencil, paperclips and stickers •

Supplies – Cork Paper: Glad Tidings; Cut Outs: EK Success, Cockadoodle Design; Stickers: Stickopotomus

SPECIAL TIPS:

Have children write their own journaling each year to see their writing skills progress over time. Leave mistakes on the layout for them to look back at in the future.

FOURTH GRADE

• create background by stitching torn purple and green patterned papers to purple patterned paper • curl top edge of bottom strip • adhere photos to background • stamp title inside die cut frame and adhere to background • print journaling onto white cardstock • highlight 'fourth grade' with pen and chalk • stitch around journaling block, double mat, roughen edges and adhere to background • stamp date onto background • punch apples from solid paper • crumple apple punches and adhere to metal-rimmed tags with colored circles • adhere to layout •

Supplies – Patterned Paper: KI Memories; Chalk: Craf-T; Die Cuts: KI Memories; Stamps: PSX; Stamp Pad: Excelsior; Tags: Avery; Punch: Carl; Font: Garamouche

How proud we are to have such a handsome, smart and enthusiastic young man for our son. Brendan couldn't wait for the first day of Fourth Grade. He was so excited! He just loves school. Even though he was going to be starting a whole new experience because he would be going to the Intermediate School this year, he just couldn't wait to get there! He was all set for his first day...wearing his new clothes and his new Nike Audacious sneakers (that he picked out himself)...and his new L.L. Bean backpack (he chose the color, Light Plum).
We are so proud of him and we hope that he always has as much enthusiasm for school and learning as he does now.

RILEY — AGE SEVEN

• create background by attaching torn notebook paper to black cardstock with white brads • double mat photo and adhere to background • attach letter stickers for title • have child handwrite journaling onto background paper • ink and crumple strip of red cardstock and attach to layout with eyelets • embellish layout with school stickers •

Supplies – Patterned Paper: Karen Foster; Cardstock: Bazzill; Stickers: Karen Foster; Ink: Colorbox; Eyelets: Making Memories

A+ Zach

• create background by adhering two torn green patterned papers and cotton binding tape to green stripe patterned paper • stamp pre-made frame with clear embossing ink, cover with deep embossing powder and heat • repeat process five times • let cool and carefully bend and crack • frame photo and adhere to background • double mat class photo and adhere to background • stamp title onto stripe paper and date onto manila library pocket • attach metal phrases with black brads, cotton string and glue dots •

Supplies – Patterned Paper: Leisure Arts; Frame: Leisure Arts; Deep Embossing Clear Powder: Suze Weinberg; Stamp: Hero Arts; Brad: Lasting Impressions; Metallic Words: DCWV

Fifth Grade Alex

• create background by adhering green patterned paper and inked brown patterned paper to brown cardstock • stamp decorative square image onto cardstock • frame photo with strips of inked brown patterned paper, fold under corners and attach to background with silver brads • reverse print title and cut out • print journaling onto clear vellum and tear and ink edges • mat journaling block with brown paper • crumple cream patterned paper and heat emboss with gold embossing powder • adhere die cut to distressed cream paper • adhere title letters to cream paper • attach journaling block with brads to die cut • frame decorator fabric with die cut frame embellished with sticker words • adhere to layout • embellish layout with brass circle clip, bookplate and brads •

Supplies – Patterned Paper: Leisure Arts; Vellum: Paper Adventure; Stamp: Stampa Rosa; Frame: Leisure Arts; Stickers: Bo Bunny; Brass Clip: Making Memories; Brads: Making Memories, All the Extras

Designer: Susan Stringfellow

TAKE 'FIVE'

• create background by adhering patterned papers to cursive patterned paper • mat one photo, roughen edges and adhere all photos to background • attach rub-on for title • print journaling onto sheet of white cardstock • highlight word with large font, chalk and pen • adhere journaling to layout • attach ruler stickers to layout • sand portion of large ruler and attach letter and number stickers • adhere mini jute to photo • embellish layout with sticker and number charm •

Supplies – Patterned Paper: 7 Gypsies, The Paper Patch; Rub-on: Making Memories; Metal Charm: Making Memories; Chalk: Craf-T; Stickers: EK Success; Font: Garamouche

6TH GRADE – FALL 98'

• create background by adhering trimmed blue patterned paper and a strip of sanded red patterned paper to blue cardstock • double mat photo with white cardstock and sanded red paper • adhere to background • reverse print title onto cardstock and cut out • stamp compass shape randomly over tag and stamp date and grade with letter stamps • mat tag with blue cardstock and attach to layout with square brad adorned with red paper • attach four eyelets to layout • tie fibers through eyelets • attach charms with silver thread •

Supplies – Patterned Paper: Leisure Arts; Stamps: Stamp Craft, Stampabilities; Eyelets: All the Extras; Concho: Scrapworks; Ink: Stampin' Up; Fiber: Fibers by the Yard; Font: Imprint MT Shadow

SPECIAL TIPS:

Alter paper by chalking, coloring, embossing, crumpling, aging, rolling, curling, folding, sanding and tearing. The possibilities are endless, so do anything and everything imaginable.

Designer: Susan Stringfellow

Madison first day of school was anticipated with the worry of meeting a new teacher and friends. Previous she had gone to Tiny Tots in the city of La Mirada but this was Pre-school! We got a new Crayola backpack with wheels(just like Mom's!) from Sam's club to make it more fun and exciting. MacKenzie, Madison and I all walked into Hillcrest school that morning. MacKenzie was ready to stay but Madison was not too sure. But when we came to pick her up at the end of the day she was all smiles. Not at all like this picture. She didn't want to come home.

SCHOOL DAYS WITH MADISON
• begin with yellow cardstock for background • double mat photo and adhere to page with corkboard photo corners • print title onto white cardstock • print journaling onto white cardstock • mat with cork paper and attach to background with brads • create pocket tag by cutting one tag in half at an angle and stitching to full tag • fill folder with school items • adhere tag to layout with ribbon •
Supplies – Ruler: Rebecca Sower

Designer: Gabrielle Mader

SPECIAL TIPS:
Create a pocket tag by cutting one tag in half at an angle and stitching it to a full tag. Fill the pocket tag with school supplies and notes from the child (it is fun to see the child's handwriting).

SCIENC club

Once a month the High Tech - High Touch Science Club stays after school for a Class. The instructor, Mr. McKinney, is real cool! Alex completed these courses: Fossil Fun, Polymer Parade, Gold Rush, Get Wired Gas Blast, & Lab 101.

LETTING MY BABY GO

• create background by adhering strip of clock patterned paper and black cardstock to yellow cardstock • adhere photo to background • print journaling onto cardstock • adhere gingham ribbon to layout • embellish with inked poetry dog tags •

Supplies – Patterned Paper: KI Memories; Cardstock: Bazzill; Ink: Staz-on

I wonder what you're doing right now and if everyone is treating you kind.
I hope there is a special person, a nice friend that you can find.
I wonder if the teacher knows just how special you are to me.
And if the brightness of your heart is something she can see.
I wonder if you are thinking about me and if you need a hug.
I already miss the sound of your voice and how you give my leg a tug.
I wonder if you could possibly understand how hard it is for me to let you grow.
On this day know that my heart breaks, for this is the first step in letting my baby go.

Alex - 8/11/2003

Designer: Jayne Hambach

HIGH TOUCH – HIGH TECH

• create background by adhering circular cuts of stripe patterned paper and torn strips of word patterned paper to brown cardstock • double mat photos and adhere to background • attach letter stickers to layout for title, name and grade • print journaling onto clear vellum and cut out • attach to layout with circle clips • scan and reduce class certificate • print onto white cardstock and attach to layout • attach fibers to layout with large circle clips and adhesive • embellish layout by drawing a primary colored border and stitching lines around edges of circles with markers •

Supplies – Patterned Paper: Leisure Arts, KI Memories; Vellum: Paper Adventures; Stickers: All the Extras, Bo Bunny, Leisure Arts; Clips: All the Extras, Work.org; Chalk: Craf-T; Fiber: Fibers by the Yard

Designer: Susan Stringfellow

makes all the difference

Books are for looks
a look for a tale
Of possibly a lion
a tiger or whale
A look for adventure
exciting intense
With mystery unfolding
and growing suspense
A look for a fact
to inform or relate
A picture a poem
or a word to locate
You never can tell
when you start to look
What interesting things
may come in a book

Designer: Stephanie Welsh

MEMBERSHIP MAKES ALL THE DIFFERENCE

• create background by adhering cut pieces of brown paper to light brown cardstock • adhere photos to background • attach letter stickers to torn white cardstock for title • print rest of title onto brown paper and tear edges • adhere title to layout • print journaling onto cardstock, tear and ink edges and adhere to layout • make book embellishments with strips of paper • round ends and accent with pen and small strips of cardstock •

Supplies – Cardstock: Bazzill; Poem: Two Peas in a Bucket; Font: Two Peas in a Bucket Vintage, AdineKirnberg Regular

HAPPINESS IS BOOKS

• begin with inked patterned paper for background • mat photo with lavender cardstock, ink edges and adhere to background • attach rub-on title to strip of coordinating patterned paper matted with cardstock • thread letter beads with wire to finish title • ink edges of title block and adhere to layout • print journaling with 2 Peas Yoyo font onto vellum • adhere journaling to layout • embellish layout with stickers •

Supplies – Patterned Paper: Chatterbox; Cardstock: Bazzill; Stickers: Sonnets; Rub-on: Making Memories; Ink: Staz-on; Font: Two Peas in a Bucket Yoyo

Designer: Shyne Hamback

PIONEER BOY

• create background by adhering red patterned paper to chalkboard patterned paper • mat photos and adhere to background • ink tags and attach letter stickers for title • attach title to background with eyelets • attach labels made from label maker to layout • mat ruler sticker with red paper and adhere to layout • ink brown bag and attach to layout with floss in corners • embellish tag with school stickers •

Supplies – Patterned Paper: Karen Foster; Stickers: Karen Foster; Tags: 2 International; Ink: Colorbok; Eyelets: Making Memories; Floss: DMC; Label Maker: Dymo

Designer: Tarri Botwinski

Designer: Sam Cousins

LEAD ME, GUIDE ME

• create background by adhering patterned paper cut into squares to blue cardstock • outline squares with pen and attach orange brads to background • triple mat photo and adhere to layout • attach letter stickers for title • print journaling onto transparency and adhere to tag • attach tag to layout over fibers with brads • embellish layout with butterfly charms •

Supplies — Patterned Paper: Leisure Arts; Metal Charms: Leisure Arts; Brads: Making Memories; Fibers: Fibers by the Yard; Font: CK Script

SCHOOL FRIENDS

• begin with white cardstock for background • size photos to frame perimeter of layout and adhere to background • cut out title from template onto blue cardstock, mat with black cardstock, cut out and adhere over mesh to blue cardstock • attach title block to background with eyelets • handwrite names of friends by photos • embellish title block with handwritten journaling and metal tag •

Supplies — Letter Template: Pagerz; Mesh: Magic Mesh

Designer: Tracy A. Weinzapfel Burges

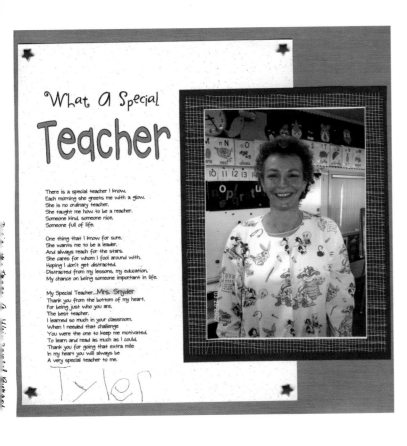

What A Special
Teacher

There is a special teacher I know.
Each morning she greets me with a glow.
She is no ordinary teacher,
She taught me how to be a reacher.
Someone kind, someone nice,
Someone full of life.

One thing that I know for sure,
She wants me to be a leader.
And always reach for the stars.
She cares for whom I fool around with,
Hoping I don't get distracted.
Distracted from my lessons, my education,
My chance on being someone important in life.

My Special Teacher...Mrs. Snyder
Thank you from the bottom of my heart,
For being just who you are,
The best teacher.
I learned so much in your classroom.
When I needed that challenge
You were the one to keep me motivated
To learn and read as much as I could,
Thank you for going that extra mile
In my heart you will always be
A very special teacher to me.

Tyler

A SPECIAL TEACHER
• begin with purple cardstock for background • enlarge photo and mat with mesh and black cardstock • print title and journaling onto cardstock and attach to background with star eyelets • cut out 'teacher' from purple cardstock and adhere to title block • highlight teachers name and have child sign bottom of poem •
Supplies – Patterned Paper: Magenta; Cardstock: Bazzill; Snaps: Making Memories; Font: Yippy Skippy; CK Handprint; CK Journaling

Ms. Parks

❋ Taught me how to read

❋ Helped me understand

❋ Let me have recess

Designer: Maegan Hall

MS. PARKS
• create background by adhering dark brown cardstock to light brown cardstock • triple mat photo with pink papers and adhere to background • print title and journaling onto white paper and cut into strips • adhere to collage of pink papers • adhere title block to layout • embellish layout with strips of pink paper, metal clip and flower stickers •
Supplies – Patterned Paper: SEI; Cardstock: Paper Garden; Clip: Making Memories; Flowers: Jolee's By You; Font: CK Girl

Hevenly   Erik Emma Natalie Brianna Jason

VDS

Hevenly

Jason

...es and one of the best things you can be. ~ Douglas Pagels

Natalie   Vanessa

Designer: Brenda Nakandakari

CLASS FRIENDS
• create background by attaching birdhouse stickers to stripe patterned paper • mat photo with torn mulberry paper and adhere to background • print journaling onto vellum and adhere to bottom of photo with vellum tape • embellish layout with stickers •

Supplies – Patterned Paper: Leisure Arts; Mulberry Paper: DCWV; Vellum: DCWV; Stickers: Leisure Arts

SCHOOL DAYS WITH SIS
• create background by adhering torn check patterned paper to purple patterned cardstock • adhere photos to background • print title with Yippy Skippy font and LD Boxed font • attach bradwear to brads for 'big' and cut out 'sis' with template • mat title with white and purple cardstock, chalk part of title • handwrite journaling and stamp date onto vellum, mat with purple cardstock, tear edges and attach to background with eyelets • embellish layout with die cuts •

Supplies – Patterned Paper: KMI; Template: Pagerz; Bradwear: Creative Imaginations; Die Cut: Sue Dreamer Doo-Dads; Fonts: Yippy Skippy, LD Boxed

Designer: Tracy A. Weinzapfel Burgos

TEACHERS GIFTS

• begin with red textured cardstock for background • mat three photos together with cardstock • double mat large photo with cardstock and wrap fiber around bottom • secure fiber with flower eyelet charm • print title onto cardstock and mat with red cardstock • print journaling onto cardstock and mat with black cardstock • adhere journaling block to background • attach title block to journaling block with circle clip •

Supplies – Cardstock: Bazzill; Fibers: On the Surface Fibers; Eyelet Flower: Making Memories; Font: First Grader

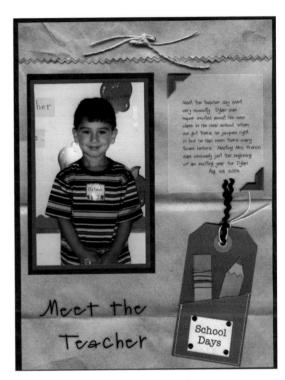

SPECIAL TIPS:

1. Center the design before trimming patterned paper from 12x12 to 8x11.
2. Trim the fibers on the tag so they don't cover the journaling.

MEET THE TEACHER

• create background by adhering trimmed patterned paper to black cardstock • double mat photo and adhere to page • attach letter stickers to layout for title • print journaling onto vellum and attach to layout with photo corners • adhere school days tag • embellish layout with fibers •

Supplies – Patterned Paper: Rebecca Sower; Cardstock: Bazzill; Tag: Rebecca Sower; Vellum: Stampin' Up; Stickers: Deluxe Cuts; Photo Corners: Making Memories

TREASURES FROM THE SEA

• create background by adhering trimmed patterned paper to cardstock • single and double mat photos and ink edges • adhere photos to background • print title onto cardstock, ink edges and stitch to background with mesh • print journaling block and strip onto cardstock • highlight journaling block words with chalk and larger font, ink edges and double mat • adhere to layout • ink edges of journaling strip and attach to layout with brads • tear piece of corrugated cardstock • stain cardstock and quotation sticker with walnut ink • spray with mist of water after ink dries to create watermarks • adhere cardboard, mesh, faux wax seal and sea glass to layout • attach quotation sticker with mini brads • embellish photo with letter sticker •

Supplies – Patterned Paper: Mustard Moon; Walnut Ink: Foofala; Faux Wax Seal: Creative Imaginations; Natural Netting: Jest Charming; Rub-on: Making Memories; Quotation: My Mind's Eye; Chalk: Craft-T; Stamp Pad: Stampin' Up; Font: Two Peas in a Bucket Jack Frost, Garamouche

ANATOMY 101

• create background by adhering blue cardstock and pieced tree and window (make to look like window in photo) to white cardstock • adhere photo to background • dress and label paper doll to match teacher in photo • print title and journaling onto cardstock, cut out and adhere to layout •

Supplies – Doll Kit: Paperkins

SPECIAL TIPS:

Use pieces of clothing from a kit to make clothes for the paper doll. Trace clothing on the backside of a piece of paper and cut out.

• begin with red patterned paper for background • mat one photo with white cardstock and trim other photo to size of overlay frame • adhere photo to underside of overlay • handwrite title and adhere to underside of overlay • print journaling and adhere to underside of overlay • adhere vellum to underside of overlay and attach overlay to background with brads • handwrite onto tags and tie to matted photo with string • trim metallic accent, double mat and adhere to layout • embellish layout with charms attached with brads and string •

Supplies – Patterned Paper: Leisure Arts; Overlay: DCWV; Charms: Leisure Arts; Adhesive: Zots; Metallic Words: DCWV

LEARNING IS FUN!

• create background by adhering school-themed fabric and ribbon to red cardstock • mat three photos with torn white cardstock • double mat main photo and tear bottom edge • print title and journaling onto vellum and tear • attach title and journaling with star eyelets •

Supplies - Fonts: David Walker, CK Girl

AGING TECHNIQUES

Aging paper is a common scrapbooking activity. The method can tie an entire layout together, and any scrapbooking element can be aged (paper, photos, stickers, accents, fibers, etc.). The scrapbooker has a variety of aging options available today.

Walnut Ink is the most popular aging medium and works very well. It is great for staining, spraying, brushing and texturing papers. Walnut ink is taken from the shells of walnuts and comes in an oily, crystallized form. To use, just add water. The color of the stain depends on how much water is used (dark–less water, light–more water). A quick and easy way to age paper is to wet paper, crumple, and dip it in the ink mixture. Leave the paper in the ink mixture longer for a darker result. If the result is too dark, the paper can be rinsed. The ink mixture can also be brushed onto paper with a foam brush or sponge. There are many ways to use the ink so experiment and have fun with it. Let the ink dry by spreading paper flat on a towel or ironing paper on a cotton setting. Walnut ink works great on most papers, but there are some that do not absorb the ink.

Acrylic Paint and Sanding can give an aged look to a variety of products. Dry brush paper with acrylic paint and let it dry. Then sand the paper for an aged look. Sanding, even without the paint, will add years to a product. Just be careful not to sand too heartily!

Tea Bag Dying is another aging option. Boil water in a pot and add a tea bag. Stain paper in a similar manner to the other water based stains.

Metallic and Luster Rub-ons are used as an aging medium as well. They have the advantage of adhering to many different materials. Rub-ons work especially well on metal and paper and can be buffed if desired. They are best applied with a finger (covered with a latex glove) or rag.

Rub n' Buff is another rub-on medium with a wax metallic finish. It works very well on metal and is long lasting. Rub n' Buff comes in a small squeezable tube and is best applied with a finger and buffed with a soft towel.

Aging Chalks work well on most papers and are easily applied with a cotton swab or make-up sponge.

Folk Antiquing Medium is a water based stain used on wood and paper alike. It comes ready to use, but can be watered down for a lighter wash.

CHRISTMAS PROGRAM

• begin with stripe patterned paper for background • frame two photos with sticker frames and mat the rest with red vellum • adhere all photos to background • adhere title sticker to background • attach letter stickers to green patterned paper for journaling • double mat and attach to background with mini snaps • mat stickers with red vellum and embellish stickers with glitter • adhere stickers to background • print vellum copy of large photo, trim smaller than actual print and attach to photo with large red snaps • attach page pebbles to sticker frame •

Supplies – Patterned Paper: Leisure Arts; Vellum: Leisure Arts; Letter Stickers: Leisure Arts; Glitter: Close to My Heart; Snaps: Making Memories; Page Pebbles: Making Memories

December 19, 2002

We had a party to celebrate the Holidays. It was so ... because SANTA CLAUS ma... surprise visit. While the ... were outside on recess ... heard sleigh bells. They ... running back into the class... where they found their stock... filled with candy and goodie... Room Moms loved seeing ... excitement in the room ... everyone emptied their stoc... and talked about hearing SA...

Designer: Camille Jensen

Hevenly, Tyler & Joshua

Stocking Time!

Hevenly & Tyler

Designer: Tracy A. Weinzapfel Burges

HOLIDAY PARTY

• create background by adhering torn and crumpled red cardstock to green cardstock • adhere photos to background • reverse print title onto green cardstock and cut out • mat title with brown cardstock, chalk edges and adhere to background • print journaling onto brown cardstock, chalk and adhere to background • embellish layout with eyelets, pre-made tag and felt stocking •

Supplies – Tag: Rebecca Sowers; Fonts: CK ClipArt, Courier New, American Classic

ORIENTAL FEAST

• create background by adhering strips of gold paper to red cardstock • mat photos, oriental images and Chinese characters and adhere to background • reverse print title with Chow Mein font, cut out and adhere to background • print journaling, mat and adhere to layout with brad • attach chopsticks to background with fishing line • adhere beads to layout • embellish layout with string, eyelets and paper animal •

Supplies – Cardstock: Bazzill; Buttons: Making Memories; Fiber: Making Memories; Beads: Westrim Crafts; Eyelets: Making Memories; Floss: DMC; Fonts: Chow Mein, Bonzai

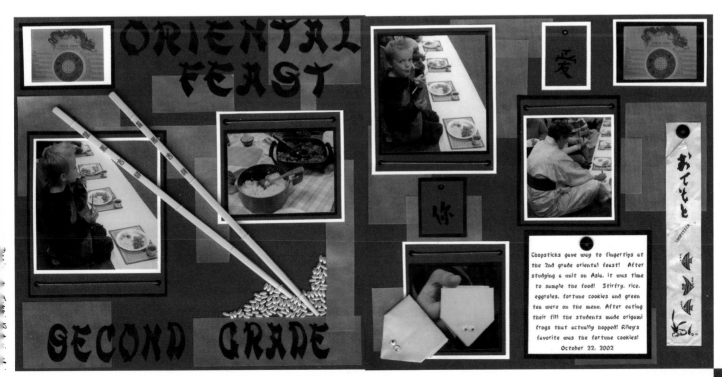

DELIGHTFULLY FRIGHTFUL HALLOWEEN

• create background by adhering four torn pieces of textured cardstock together • adhere torn green strip to background • frame two photos and purple cardstock with sticker frames • mat third photo and sticker frames with cardstock • adhere photos to background • attach stickers to orange patterned paper for title, punch into circles and attach title to layout with brass and silver circles • stamp journaling onto drafting paper, tear edges and mat with torn mulberry paper • attach to page with embroidery floss • create 'parade' by painting tags with yellow acrylic paint • attach letter stickers and heat emboss several times with clear embossing powder • attach to sticker frame with purple floss • create ghost shrinky dinks with ghost stamps and ink • embellish layout with Halloween buttons, floss and stickers matted with cardstock and torn mulberry paper • Supplies – Patterned Paper: Leisure Arts; Cardstock: Bazzill; Stickers: Leisure Arts; Sticker Frames: Leisure Arts; Stamp: DJ Inkers, Imaginations; Ink: Staz-on; Embossing Powder: Suze Weinberg; Brads: Scrapworks; Silver Circles: Scrapworks

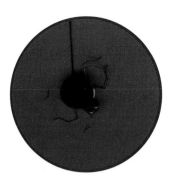

SPIDERMAN HALLOWEEN

• begin with red cardstock for background • draw web pattern onto background • hermafix back of cardstock • punch holes every 1/8" to 1/4" to form outline of web • stitch web with needle and floss • single and double mat photos and adhere to background • print title onto red cardstock, mat with black cardstock and adhere to background • adhere spider to web •
Supplies – Floss: DMC; Stickers: Jolee's; Font: 1979

Designer: Tracy A. Weinzapfel Burgos

COSTUME PARADE

• create background by adhering patterned paper to gold cardstock • mat photos with gold cardstock and adhere to background • stamp title and journaling onto background • embellish layout with Halloween stickers •
Supplies – Patterned Paper: Leisure Arts; Stickers: Leisure Arts

Designer: Jane Swanson

EVERY CHILD IS AN ARTIST
• create background by adhering check patterned paper and trimmed pink cardstock to blue cardstock • attach photos to background with black photo corners • scan and print two copies of child's drawing and double mat with pink and blue cardstocks • create title with letter stickers and printed transparency • adhere title to background • print journaling onto transparency • adhere to blue patterned tag • adhere tag to layout • adhere fiber to layout with glue dots to simulate the flow of watercolors • adhere paintbrush to layout • embellish layout with sticker dots •
Supplies – Patterned Paper: Provo Craft; Stickers: Renae Lindgren; Photo Corners: Canson; Fiber: Fibers by the Yard

SPECIAL TIPS:
Attach fiber to layout where it falls to give a natural look.

Designer: Tracy A. Weinzapfel Burgos

EASTER 'EGG'SPERTS

• begin with patterned paper for background • mat four photos and adhere all photos to background • reverse print title onto patterned paper, cut out, outline with black pen and mat with pink cardstock • handwrite journaling onto green cardstock and attach stickers to green cardstock • outline journaling and sticker block with black pen and mat with pink cardstock • adhere title, journaling and sticker blocks to layout • embellish layout with stickers, tags and string •

Supplies – Patterned Paper: Creative Memories; Templates: EK Success, Deluxe Cuts; Stickers: Stickopotomus

Designer: Brenda Nakandakari

LITTLE ARTIST

• create background by adhering trimmed white cardstock to black cardstock • adhere photos to background • print title and journaling onto white cardstock, chalk edges and use water brush to run chalked colors together • adhere title and journal blocks to background • attach heart eyelets to background • string matching ribbon through each set of eyelets •

Supplies – Fonts: CK Artisan, DJ Crayon, Book Antiqua

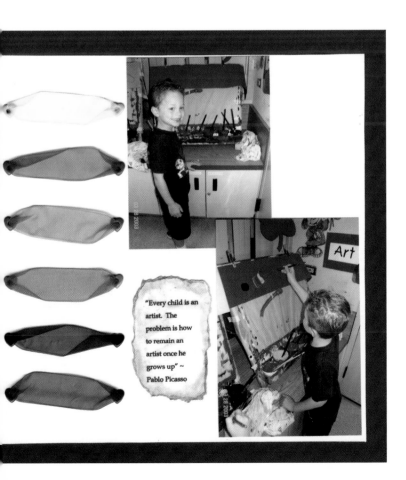

FEILD DAY 2003

• create background by stitching green patterned paper and mesh to brown cardstock with floss • frame and mat photos • handwrite title onto smooth side of clear shrinky dink with black pen • draw a border with pen onto each shrinky dink • stamp journaling onto cardstock and mat • texture torn water colored paper with a stamp and three different color ink pads • ink paper in a striped pattern • stamp flowers along bottom of water colored paper • punch out three flowers to use as reverse stencil • temporarily adhere to water colored paper and sponge around each flower with different colors • remove stencil and adhere water colored paper to background • attach black brads to the center of flowers • adhere title and journaling to layout • adhere and attach photos to layout with brads • embellish layout with waxy floss •
Supplies – Patterned Paper: Leisure Arts; Mesh: Magenta; Metal Frames: DCWV

WILDLIFE

• create background by adhering strips of green cardstock to light green cardstock • mat three photos with cardstock and corrugated cardboard and adhere to background • attach letter stickers to inked and matted cardstock for title • finish title by reverse printing letters onto brown cardstock, cut out and adhere to torn and inked cardstock • adhere title to background • print journaling onto cardstock, ink and cut to form tags • adhere to layout • embellish layout with fiber and an eyelet •

Supplies – Paper: Serendipity Paper; Stickers: David Walker; Chalk: Craf-T; Fiber: On The Surface; Eyelet: HyGlo; Fonts: Dreamer One, American Typewriter

Designer: Betsy Sammarco

ANIMALS ON THE RANCH

• create background by adhering torn and chalked cardstock to white cardstock • single and double mat photos • tear and chalk bottom edge of one photo • trace letters with template, cut out and mat with black cardstock for title • attach title to background with eyelets as center of letters • print rest of title and journaling onto white cardstock • tear and chalk edges • attach title block to layout with eyelets • adhere journaling block to background • embellish layout with jute and buttons •

Supplies – Cardstock: Bazzill; Button: Dress it Up; Twistal: Making Memories

Designer: Tracy A. Weinzapfel Burgos

Designer: Camille Jensen

POSTING THE COLORS

• create background by adhering distressed paper to tan cardstock • create distressed paper by crumpling, running under water and soaking tan cardstock in walnut ink for one minute • let paper dry and lightly sponge upper left corner with blue paint in a rectangle • apply ink to rectangle with a blue ink pad and fingers • stamp stars onto the blue rectangle with white pigment ink • lightly wash paper with walnut ink and rub in red ink stripes • mat photos with tan cardstock with inked and roughened edges • adhere photos to background with inked metal cut into photo corners • tie red waxy floss around each corner • print title and journaling onto transparency • mat journaling with red vellum and blue pinstriped paper • sew title, journaling and silver tags to background with red waxy floss •

Supplies – Patterned Paper: Leisure Arts, 7 Gypsies; Cardstock: DCWV; Ink: Staz-on

Designer: Tracy A. Weinzapfel Burgos

FIELD DAY

• create background by adhering trimmed and torn blue and yellow patterned paper to black cardstock • single and double mat photos and adhere to background • reverse print title onto white cardstock, cut out and adhere to background • attach letter stickers to background to finish title • print journaling onto vellum and adhere to tag made from torn cardstock • punch four holes across top of tag and weave fibers through holes • adhere tag to layout • print date onto vellum and attach to layout with a circle clip •

Supplies – Patterned Paper: Making Memories, Colorbok; Cardstock: Making Memories; Vellum: Paper Adventures; Stickers: All the Extras; Circle Clips: All the Extras; Fiber: Fibers by the Yard; Font: Rausch

Designer: Susan Stringfellow

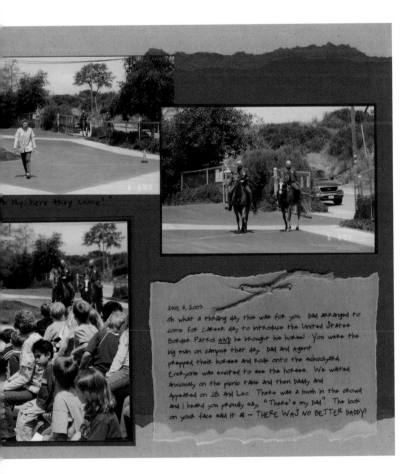

CAREER DAY

• create background by adhering torn brown cardstock to tan cardstock • attach gold eyelets to brown cardstock and lace twine over gap • single and double mat some photos • cut out title using template, mat and adhere to background • print journaling onto vellum • tear and chalk edges • attach to background with eyelets and twine • handwrite journaling next to photos •

Supplies – Letter Template: Provo Craft; Font: Janelleshand

Designer: Tarri Botwinski

THINK, STUDY, LEARN
• create background by adhering scanned and lightened worksheet of child's homework to black cardstock • triple mat photo and adhere to layout • reverse print title and cut out letters • adhere to background • print journaling onto cardstock, cut out and attach to layout with eyelets • attach eyelets to layout • string fiber and wire through eyelets • embellish layout with star buttons threaded with wire •
Supplies – Cardstock: Bazzill; Fiber: Making Memories; Buttons: Dress It Up; Eyelets: Making Memories; Wire: Fiber Creations; Font: Marydale, Beach

Homework

Designer: Tracy A. Weinzapfel Burgos

Room **mom**

I had the special privilege to be Room Mom this year. I coordinated parties, carnivals, etc. and helped Mrs. Snyder any way I could. I also had the pleasure of **volunteering** in the classroom every Friday. With the twins in tow I would assist Mrs. Snyder with lessons, recess, and daily activities.

I learned a lot on those Fridays. First I learned that teaching is exhausting but **rewarding**. I enjoyed watching the bond Mrs. Snyder had with the kids and their parents. I too formed a **bond** with her and the kids. I got to work with the "Red Bears" group that included Tyler, Emma, Carter, Vincent, and Lauren. It was fun to sit there and "*teach*" them during the various activities Mrs. Snyder had laid out for us. Then we would do a class art project, which was my *favorite*. Kindergarten crafts are so much **fun**! Finally I would help supervise recess which the twins **LOVED**. This gave me the chance to talk to Mrs. Snyder. It was my chance to always stay on top of Tyler's progress and behavior.

Being Room Mom is an unpaid job but very **rewarding** in so many ways. I got to see Tyler *interacting* with his friends. When there was a bruised knee that required a Mommy's touch or a trip to the nurse I was there. When there were disagreements I got to play referee. Other moms would ask how I did it with the twins and all but I saw that making Tyler a **priority** meant a lot to him. I also got to know Mrs. Snyder as a teacher and **friend**.

Overall, I would say my first year as Room Mom was *successful* and fun. Being at home allotted me this opportunity and I am so *thankful* for it. I once had a friend tell me that no paycheck can beat that and she was so right. I center my world around my kids and I hope they **benefit** from it.

ASSESSMENT REPORT

• create background by adhering piece of textured cardstock to green patterned paper forming a pocket • adhere photo to background • reverse print title and cut out • adhere to vellum with window cut to show photo • handwrite school name and year onto vellum for journaling • embellish layout with fibers attached with gold brads • place report card in pocket •

Supplies – Patterned Paper: Provo Craft; Cardstock: Bazzill; Punch: Paper Shapers; Font: LD Chicken Scratch

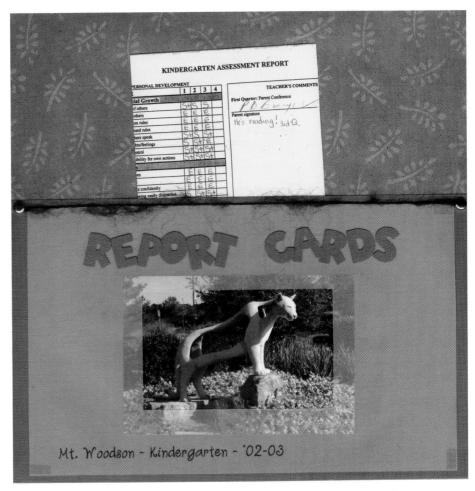

Mt. Woodson ~ Kindergarten ~ '02-03

Designer: Tracy A. Weinzapfel Burgos

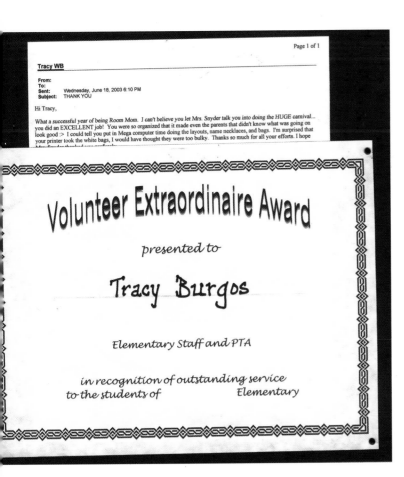

VOLUNTEER EXTRAORDINAIRE

• begin with black cardstock for background • print journaling onto piece of white paper and adhere to background • attach swirl stickers for title • adhere photo to layout • create pocket from school award attached to background with black brads • put party-coordinating information into pocket • remove shanks from heart buttons and hang with floss • adhere hearts and floss to layout •

Supplies – Stickers: David Walker; Floss: DMC; Buttons: Dress it Up; Alphawear: Creative Imaginations; Font: LD Cool

Designer: Susan Stringfellow

Classic Alex

Alex was excited to wear my letter jacket for 50's Grandparents Day at school.

November '99

CLASSIC ALEX

• create background by adhering trimmed brown cardstock and strip of black and white checked paper to black cardstock • double mat photo and adhere to background • reverse print title onto black cardstock and cut out • adhere title to layout • print journaling, date and border words onto clear vellum • attach journaling to layout with mini silver brads • scan and reduce sheet music and print onto white cardstock • create border squares by matting four punched squares of sheet music paper with black cardstock • mat four white circles with black cardstock • attach border words and circles to squares with silver eyelets • adhere completed squares to checked border • attach date to layout with black eyelet •
Supplies – Vellum: Paper Adventures; Brads: Making Memories; Eyelets: Making Memories; Font: Harlow

CLIMB HIGH, CLIMB FAR

• create background by adhering blocks of vellum, mesh and patterned paper to blue cardstock • tear one edge of each photo, color with watercolor crayons and adhere to background • attach sticker letters to background for title • adhere vellum quotes to layout • color leaves onto vellum with watercolor crayons • crackle center block of vellum and paint with acrylic paint • blend colors with a watercolor crayon • print words onto twill tape and attach to layout with black brads • adhere beads to layout • embellish layout with stickers, keys, fiber, circle clips and bookplates •
Supplies – Patterned Paper: Creative Imaginations, My Mind's Eye; Vellum: Autumn Leaves; Mesh: Magenta; Stamps: Hero Arts; Brads: American Tag Company; Bookplates: Two Peas in a Bucket; Quotes: Memories Complete; Beads: Magic Scraps; Title: Making Memories; Stickers: EK Success; Swirl Clips: Boxer Productions; Acrylic Paint: Delta; Font: Two Peas in a Bucket Flea Market

Believe Dream Climb Soar Believe Dream Climb Soar

climb high, climb far, your goal the sky your aim the star.

Williams College Inscription

Matt 9

nobody knows what a boy is worth, and the world must wait and see; for every man in an honored place, is a boy that used to be

- Phillips Brooks

NOBODY KNOWS

• create background by adhering strips of cardstock to green cardstock • mat one photo with cardstock and square punch other photos • frame one small photo with a metal frame • print title and journaling directly onto background cardstock • print quote onto tan cardstock, tear bottom edge and double mat • adhere to background over torn circle of cardstock • adhere photos to layout with three small photos over a torn oval of cardstock • embellish layout with metal snaps and jute •
Supplies – Metal Frame: Making Memories; Metal Snaps: Making Memories; Metal Letter: Making Memories

Scanning photos and images into a computer opens up a world of possibilities for the scrapbooker. Once a photo has been scanned, photos can be altered in a photo software program or sent to family and friends over the Internet. Scanning is not a difficult process:

1. Place item to be scanned face down on glass.

2. Select the area you want to be scanned.

3. Check the settings.

    a. Keep the resolution at a minimum of 300 DPI (Dots Per Inch).

    b. Scan the image size larger or equivalent to the size you want to print.

4. Scan the item.

5. Save the file.

    a. JPEG files are the most common for emailing since they are the most Internet compatible.

    b. TIFF files are the best option for altering images in design programs and printing high quality prints.

Enjoy altering your photos and images on the computer; just remember that it takes some patience and work to get the same color tones you see on your screen to appear on the printed photo.

Designer: Jayne Hanback

ALEX 2003

WORDS

COULD NOT

EXPRESS

JUST HOW MUCH

I

LOVE

YOU

WORDS COULD NOT EXPRESS

• create background by adhering inked dictionary paper to cursive patterned paper • ink edges of large photo, stamp name and year to photo and adhere to background • tear edges of small photo, mod-podge and mat with sheet of used fabric softener and black cardstock • adhere photo to layout • mod-podge word stickers for title and adhere to layout • stamp letters to finish title • punch square of dictionary patterned paper, mat with black paper and attach to large photo with red heart eyelet • embellish layout with matted metal heart •

Supplies – Patterned Paper: Mustard Moon, 7 Gypsies; Ink: Staz-on; Metal Heart: Making Memories

Men of Character

Char-ac-ter (noun). 1. trait. 2. moral quality and integrity. 3. Good repute.

Our dearest children, we vow to raise you to be men of good character with strong family values. Always remember to love and support each other, trust God in all things, and seek first to understand and then to be understood.

Designer: Leah Fung

WHERE HAS THE TIME GONE?

• begin with patterned paper for background • double mat large photo with cardstock and frame small photo with a metal frame • adhere photos to background • print title and journaling onto transparency and adhere to background • embellish layout with fibers, metal hearts, Chinese coins and a clock piece adhered to a black slide •

Supplies – Patterned Paper: Club Scrap; Chinese Coins: All the Extras; Fiber: Fibers by the Yard; Charm: All the Extras; Watch: All the Extras; Metal Slide: Making Memories; Fonts: Two Peas in a Bucket Stamp Act, Two Peas in a Bucket Hot Chocolate

WHERE HAS THE TIME GONE?

I keep looking at you and asking myself this very question. How can you be 13 years old now? I remember so clearly when I was pregnant with you and I remember the day I delivered you and the happiness that flooded my heart the minute I saw you. It seems like just yesterday I was feeding you a bottle and watching you roll over for the first time. Now you are so grown up. You now have a dry sense of humor you are an honor roll student and an outstanding Goalie in hockey. I just want you to know that you have brought so much happiness and joy into my life and being a mother is the best thing that has ever happened to me. I feel so blessed by God to be given the chance to your mom. I love you with all my heart and you will always be my little Scotty. I heard this saying recently and I want you to remember it from me because I believe this and I want you to. "Remember in life it is nice to be important but it is more important to be nice." Love Mom April 18, 2003

Val-ues (noun). 1. ideals or principles. 2. to regard highly.

Value the things in life that really matter such as family, faith in God, and integrity.

MEN OF CHARACTER

• create background by adhering trimmed patterned paper to black cardstock • mat large photo with cardstock, corrugated paper and pleated suede • adhere all photos to layout • print journaling onto red patterned paper and tear one edge • sew small journaling block to patterned and corrugated paper • adhere journaling blocks to layout • adhere die cuts to large journaling block for title • embellish journaling blocks with strips of checked paper, snaps and an alphabet eyelet •

Supplies – Patterned Paper: K & Company, Making Memories; Snaps: Making Memories; Title: Quickutz

Creating a great scrapbook page can become a whole lot easier if you have the right tools and equipment. We asked some of our best designers to give us a list of the scrapbooking tools they could not live without. Here is their list:

1. BUTTONS
2. CARDSTOCK
3. EYELET TOOL
4. FIBERS
5. METAL ACCENTS
6. PAPER TRIMMER
7. WALNUT INK
8. WIRE
9. MESH

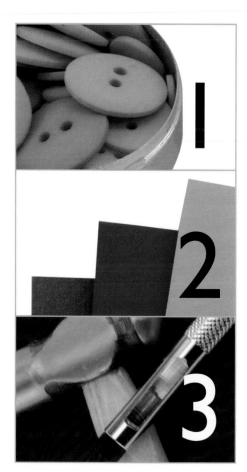

SOURCES

The following companies manufacture products featured in this book. Please check with your local retail store for these materials. We have made every attempt to identify and give proper credit for the materials used in this book. If by chance we have missed giving the appropriate credit, we would appreciate hearing from you.

3L Corp.
(800) 828-3130 3lcorp.com

3M Stationary
(800) 364-3577 3m.com

7-Gypsies
(800) 588 6707 7gypsies.com

Accu-Cut Systems
(800) 288-1670 accucut.com

American Tag Company
(800) 223-3956 americantag.net

Amscan
(800) 284-4333 amscan.com

Artistic Wire
(630) 530-7567 artisticwire.com

Bazzill
(480) 558-8557 bazzillbasics.com

Bo-Bunny Press
(801) 771-4010 bobunny.com

Boxer Scrapbook Productions, LLC
(888) 625-6255 or (503) 625-0455
boxerscrapbooks.com

Canson, Inc.
(800) 628-9283 canson-us.com

Carl Mfg. USA, Inc.
(800) 257-4771 carl-products.com

Chatterbox, Inc.
(888) 416-6260 chatterboxinc.com

Close to My Heart
Closetomyheart.com

Coats & Clark
coatsandclark.com

Cock-A-Doodle Design, Inc.
(800) 262-9727
cockadoodledesign.com

Colorbok
(800) 366-4660 colorbok.com

Craf-T Products
(800) 530-3410 craf-tproducts.com

Crafter's Workshop, The
(877) CRAFTER thecraftersworkshop.com

Creative Imaginations
(800) 942-6487 cigift.com
Creative Memories

(800) 341-5275
creativememories.com

Cut-It-Up
(530) 389-2233 cut-it-up.com

Darice
(800) 426-4659 darice.com

DCWV
(801) 224-6766 diecutswithaview.com

Decoart
(606) 365-3193 decoart.com

Delta Crafts
(800) 423-4135 deltacrafts.com

Deluxe Cuts
(480) 497-9005 deluxecuts.com

Design Originals
d-originals.com

DJ Inkers
Djinkers.com

DMC
(973) 589-0606 dmc-usa.com

Dress It Up
dressitup.com

DYMO
(800) 426-7827 dymo.com

EK Success
(800) 524-1349 eksuccess.com

Fibers by the Yard
fibersbytheyard.com

Fiber Creations
(770) 965-0018 bjsfibercreations.com

FiberScraps
(215) 230-4905 fiberscraps.com

FoofaLa
(402) 758-0863 foofala.com

Frances Meyer
francesmeyer.com

Herma Fix
Herma.co.uk.com

Hero Art Rubber Stamps, Inc.
(800) 822-4376 hearoarts.com

Hobby Lobby
Hobbylobby.com

HyGlo Crafts
(480) 968-6475 hyglocrafts.com

Imaginations, Inc.
(801) 225-6015 imaginations-inc.com

Jest Charming
(702) 564-5101 jestcharming.com

Karen Foster Design
(801) 451-9779
karenfosterdesign.com

Keeping Memories Alive
(800) 419-4949 scrapbooks.com

KI Memories
(469) 633-9665 kimemories.com

Leave Memories
Leavememories.com

Leisure Arts
(888) 257-7548
business.leisurearts.com

Li'l Davis Designs
(949) 838-0344 lildavisdesigns.com

Magenta Rubber Stamps
Magentarubberstamps.com

Magic Mesh
(651) 345-6374 magicmesh.com

Magic Scraps
(972) 238-1838 magicscraps.com

Making Memories
(800) 286-5263 makingmemories.com

Me and My Big Ideas
(949) 589-4607 meandmybigideas.com

Memories Complete
(888)966-6365
memoriescomplete.com

Michael's
(800) 642-4235 michaels.com

Mrs. Grossman's
(800) 429-4549 mrsgrossmans.com

Mustard Moon
(408) 229-8542 mustardmoon.com

My Minds Eye
Frame-ups.com

Offray & Son, Inc.
Offray.com

On the Surface
(847) 675-2520

Paper Adventures
(800) 727-0699 paperadventures.com

Paper Bliss
Paperbliss.com

Paper Garden
papergarden.com

Paper Patch
Paperpatch.com

Provo Craft
(888) 577-3545 provocraft.com

PSX
(800) 782-6748 psxdesign.com

Quickutz
(888) 702-1146 quickutz.com

Scrapworks, LLC
scrapworksllc.com

SEI, Inc.
(800) 333-3279 shopsei.com

Serendipity Stamps
(816) 532-0740
serendipitystamps.com

Stampabilities
(800) 888-0321 stampabilities.com

Stamp Craft
(08) 8941 1066 stampcraft.com

Sticker Studio
Stickerstudio.com

The Robin's Nest
(435) 789-5387 robinsnest-scrapbook.com

Two Peas In A Bucket
twopeasinabucket.com

Un-Du
Un-du.com

Westrim Crafts
(800) 727-2727 westrimcrafts.com

Xyron
(800) 793-3523 xyron.com

Look for these published or soon to be published
Leisure Arts Scrapbooking Idea Books

IT'S ALL IN YOUR IMAGINATION

IT'S ALL ABOUT BABY

IT'S ALL ABOUT TECHNIQUE

IT'S ALL ABOUT CARDS AND TAGS

IT'S ALL ABOUT PETS

IT'S ALL ABOUT TRAVEL

IT'S ALL ABOUT HERITAGE PAGES

IT'S ALL ABOUT TEENS

IT'S ALL ABOUT STEP-SAVING DESIGNS

Instructions for back cover:

SCHOOL IS OUT

• begin with blue patterned paper for background • enlarge photo and mat with green patterned paper • apply a pre-colored crystal lacquer along edge of photo • let dry for three hours • attach photo to background over blue mesh with cross stitches and embroidery floss • print title onto transparency • attach to background over metal strips with green eyelets and black brads • attach letter stickers to large metal rimmed tag • attach to background over blue mesh with large blue brad • stamp names and grade on metal-rimmed tags and attach to layout with large brads • stamp date onto metal tag and attach to photo with black brad •
Supplies – Patterned Paper: Leisure Arts; Stickers: Leisure Arts; Tags: Making Memories; Stamp: Hero Arts; Stamp Pad: Staz-on; Font: CK Constitution, CK Newspaper